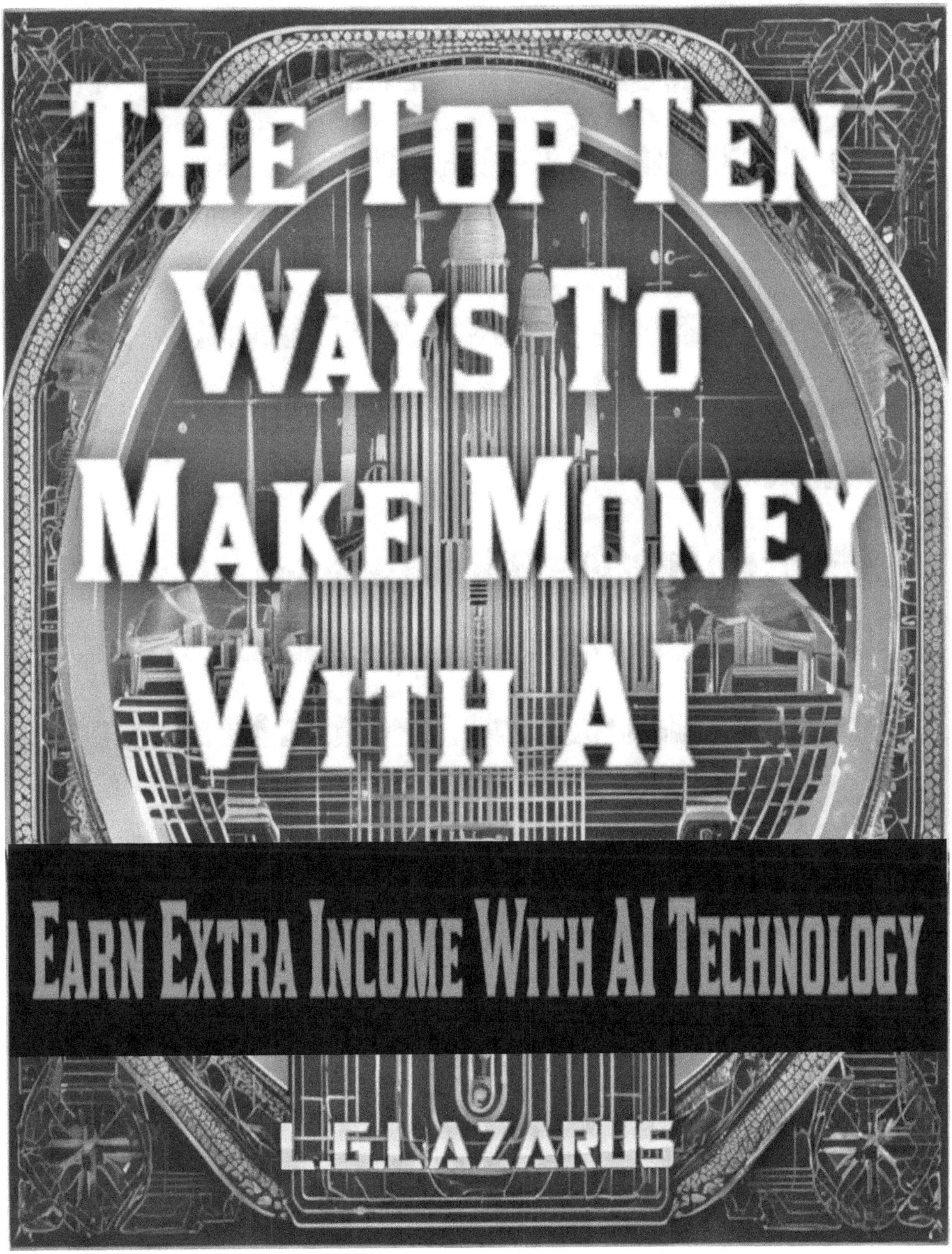
THE TOP TEN
WAYS TO
MAKE MONEY
WITH AI
EARN EXTRA INCOME WITH AI TECHNOLOGY
L.G.LAZARUS

Table of Contents

Introduction: Overview of AI's Potential

Chapter 1: Building AI-Powered Applications

Chapter 2: Selling AI-Driven Services

Chapter 3: Creating and Selling AI Content

Chapter 4: Developing AI Courses and Educational Materials

Chapter 5: Investing in AI Startups and Technologies

Chapter 6: Leveraging AI for E-Commerce

Chapter 7: Monetizing AI-Generated Art and Media

Chapter 8: Developing Niche AI Tools

Chapter 9: Using AI for Stock Market Analysis and Trading

Chapter 10: Offering AI Automation for Businesses

Copyright © 2024 by L.G.Lazarus

Introduction: Overview of AI's Potential

Artificial Intelligence (AI) has rapidly transformed from a futuristic concept into an integral part of our daily lives. It is a field of computer science that focuses on creating systems capable of performing tasks that would typically require human intelligence. These tasks include learning, reasoning, problem-solving, perception, and even creativity. From virtual assistants like Siri and Alexa to complex systems driving autonomous vehicles and powering medical diagnostics, AI is shaping the world around us in profound ways.

What is Artificial Intelligence?

At its core, AI refers to the simulation of human intelligence processes by machines, especially computer systems. It encompasses several branches, including:

- **Machine Learning (ML):** Systems that learn and improve from experience without being explicitly programmed.
- **Natural Language Processing (NLP):** The ability of machines to understand and respond to human language.
- **Computer Vision:** Enabling machines to interpret and analyze visual information from the world.
- **Robotics:** The integration of AI into machines to perform tasks autonomously.

AI is not limited to theoretical research—it has become a practical tool driving innovation and economic growth across industries.

Current Trends and Advancements in AI Technology

The rapid evolution of AI technology has led to remarkable advancements that are reshaping industries:

- **Generative AI:** Tools like ChatGPT and DALL·E enable the creation of text, images, and even music, opening new avenues in creativity and content generation.
- **AI in Healthcare:** AI-powered diagnostics, personalized medicine, and robotic surgeries are improving health outcomes globally.
- **AI in Finance:** Predictive algorithms and fraud detection systems are revolutionizing the financial sector.
- **Automation in Business:** From customer service chatbots to automated data analysis, AI is streamlining operations and reducing costs.
- **AI in Entertainment:** AI is being used to create hyper-personalized recommendations, produce realistic special effects, and even compose original music and scripts.

These trends are fueled by the increasing availability of data, advancements in computational power, and the proliferation of accessible AI tools and platforms.

Why AI is a Lucrative Avenue for Entrepreneurs and Professionals

The business potential of AI is immense, making it one of the most promising fields for generating income and driving innovation. Here's why:

1. **High Demand Across Industries:** Companies in healthcare, finance, retail, and beyond are investing heavily in AI to gain competitive advantages.
2. **Scalability:** AI solutions can often be scaled globally, turning local innovations into worldwide success stories.
3. **Cost Efficiency:** By automating repetitive tasks, AI reduces labor costs and increases efficiency, making it highly attractive for businesses.
4. **Endless Opportunities:** The versatility of AI allows entrepreneurs to create solutions for diverse problems, from improving customer service to optimizing supply chains.
5. **Early Adoption Advantage:** While AI is rapidly growing, it's still in a relatively early stage, meaning entrepreneurs and professionals who adopt AI now can position themselves as pioneers in this transformative field.

AI is not just a tool for tech-savvy individuals; it's a democratized resource that can empower anyone with creativity and drive to turn ideas into profitable ventures. Whether you're a seasoned entrepreneur or someone exploring new career opportunities, leveraging AI can unlock unprecedented possibilities for growth and success.

In this book, we will explore ten practical and innovative ways to harness the power of AI to generate income, making it accessible for everyone willing to step into this exciting frontier.

How to Use This Book

This book is your roadmap to leveraging the transformative power of Artificial Intelligence (AI) to create profitable ventures and enhance your professional pursuits. Whether you're an experienced entrepreneur, a tech enthusiast looking to explore new opportunities, or a business-minded individual curious about AI, this book is designed to meet you where you are and guide you toward success.

Structure and Purpose

The book is divided into ten chapters, each focusing on a specific way to make money with AI. The structure is straightforward, practical, and action-oriented:

1. **Introduction to Each Opportunity:**
   Each chapter begins with an explanation of a particular AI-based income stream. You'll learn how it works, its applications, and its potential for profit.
2. **Step-by-Step Guidance:**
   Practical steps are outlined to help you get started, even if you have no prior experience with AI. From tools to resources, you'll find everything you need to take the first step.
3. **Real-World Examples:**
   Case studies and success stories illustrate how others have achieved results, providing inspiration and actionable insights.

1. **Challenges and Solutions:**
   Every opportunity comes with its own set of challenges. This book addresses common obstacles and offers solutions to help you overcome them.
2. **Scaling and Long-Term Growth:**
   Each chapter concludes with tips for scaling your efforts and maximizing your earning potential.

At the end of the book, you'll find additional resources, including a glossary of AI terms and recommended tools, to further support your journey.

Who This Book Is For

This book is written with a broad audience in mind, ensuring accessibility and value for readers of all backgrounds:

- **Entrepreneurs:** If you're looking to start or expand a business, this book will show you how to integrate AI into your operations or create entirely new ventures.
- **Tech Enthusiasts:** If you're fascinated by AI but unsure how to turn your interest into income, this book will provide clear pathways to do so.
- **Business-Minded Individuals:** Whether you're an executive, freelancer, or someone exploring side hustles, you'll discover how AI can streamline operations, boost efficiency, and unlock new revenue streams.
- **Beginners and Experts Alike:** No prior knowledge of AI is required. The book starts with the basics and progressively delves into more advanced concepts, ensuring that everyone can benefit.

How to Approach This Book

You don't have to read the book in order. Feel free to jump to chapters that interest you the most. Each chapter is self-contained, so you can focus on the opportunities that resonate with your skills and interests.

By the end of this book, you'll have a clear understanding of how to harness AI to create meaningful income streams and potentially transform your career or business. Let's dive in and unlock the wealth of possibilities AI has to offer!

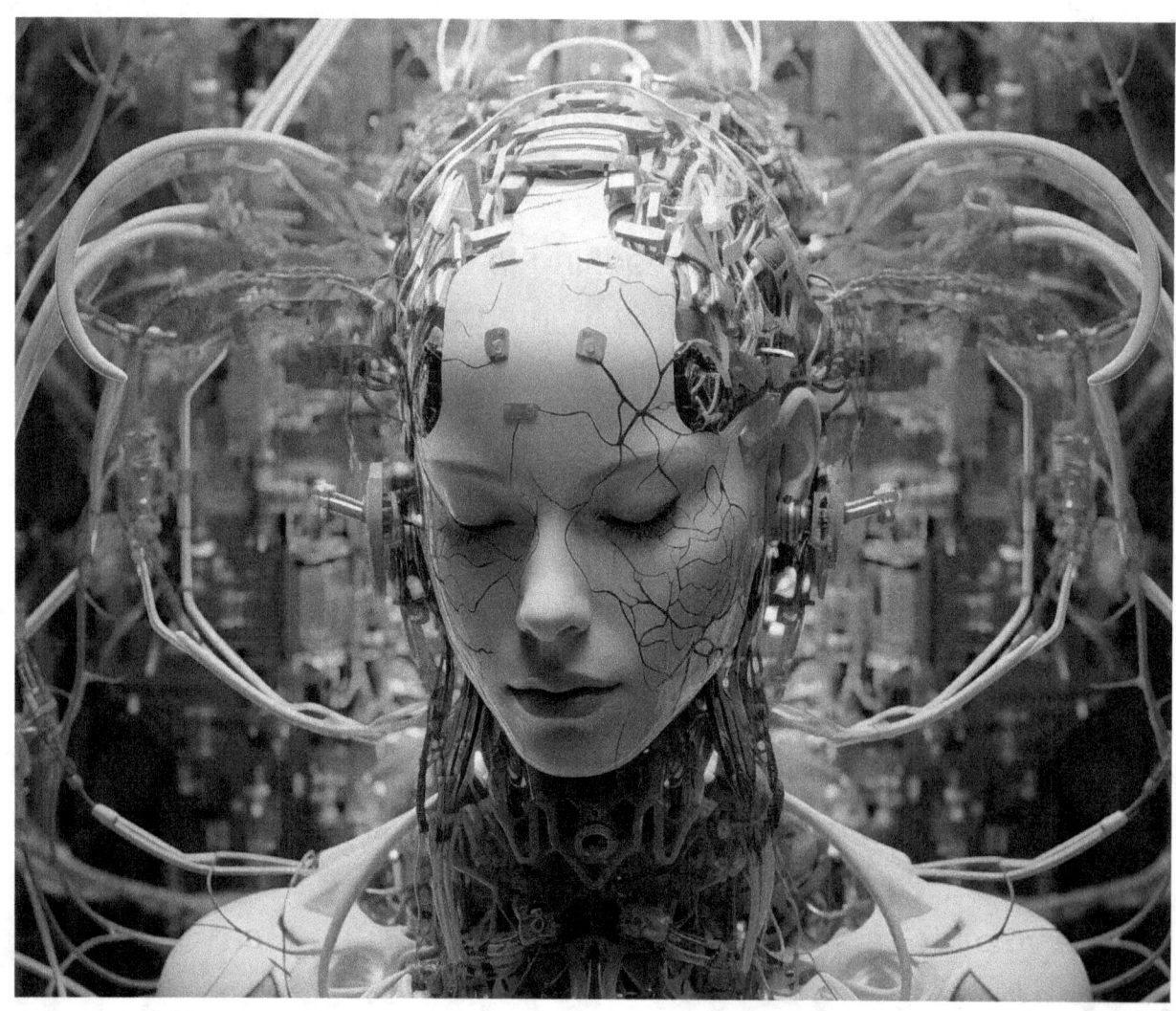

Chapter 1: Chapter 1: Building AI-Powered Applications

The rise of Artificial Intelligence has created countless opportunities for developing innovative applications that solve real-world problems and generate significant revenue. Whether you're a seasoned developer or a beginner with an idea, creating AI-powered applications is one of the most lucrative and impactful ways to capitalize on the AI revolution.

Introduction to AI App Development

AI app development involves creating software applications that leverage Artificial Intelligence technologies to perform intelligent tasks. These applications use techniques such as machine learning, natural language processing, and computer vision to analyze data, make predictions, and provide personalized experiences for users.

Why are AI-powered applications so valuable? The answer lies in their ability to:

- **Automate repetitive tasks:** Reducing human effort and error.
- **Personalize user experiences:** Delivering tailored recommendations and services.
- **Enhance decision-making:** Analyzing vast amounts of data for actionable insights.

With demand for AI solutions surging across industries, developers who can build AI-powered applications are poised to thrive.

Examples of Successful AI Applications

Many well-known companies have harnessed AI to create transformative applications. Here are some notable examples:

1. **Chatbots and Virtual Assistants**
    - **Examples:** ChatGPT, Siri, Alexa, and Google Assistant.
    - **Impact:** Automate customer service, enhance user engagement, and provide 24/7 support.
2. **Recommendation Engines**
    - **Examples:** Netflix's personalized viewing suggestions, Amazon's product recommendations, and Spotify's Discover Weekly playlists.
    - **Impact:** Increase customer satisfaction and drive sales by delivering highly relevant suggestions.
3. **Image and Speech Recognition Apps**
    - **Examples:** Face recognition in Apple's Face ID, Google Photos, and AI transcription tools like Otter.ai.
    - **Impact:** Revolutionize security, accessibility, and content creation.
4. **Healthcare Applications**
    - **Examples:** AI systems for medical imaging (e.g., detecting tumors in X-rays) and personalized health tracking apps like Fitbit.
    - **Impact:** Save lives, improve healthcare access, and streamline medical processes.
5. **AI in Gaming**
    - **Examples:** AI opponents in video games and personalized gaming experiences using machine learning.
    - **Impact:** Enhance user immersion and challenge levels in games.

These applications showcase the diverse opportunities AI offers for developers to create value across multiple sectors.

Tools and Resources for Beginners and Experts

Building AI-powered applications has never been more accessible, thanks to a wide range of tools and platforms available for developers of all skill levels. Here are some essential resources:

1. Frameworks and Libraries

- **TensorFlow:** A versatile open-source library for machine learning and AI development.
- **PyTorch:** Popular among researchers for its flexibility and ease of use in creating neural networks.
- **Scikit-learn:** Ideal for beginners working on machine learning projects.

2. Platforms for Building AI Models

- **Google AI Platform:** Provides tools for developing, training, and deploying AI models.
- **AWS AI Services:** Amazon's suite of AI and machine learning tools for application development.
- **Microsoft Azure AI:** Offers pre-built AI models and tools for custom solutions.

3. No-Code and Low-Code Platforms

- **RunwayML:** Enables creators to build AI-powered apps and tools without extensive coding knowledge.
- **Bubble:** A no-code platform for designing and deploying AI-enhanced web applications.

- **Zapier + OpenAI Integration:** Automate workflows with AI capabilities.

4. Data Sources and APIs

- **OpenAI API:** Access state-of-the-art language models like GPT for integration into your apps.
- **Google Cloud Vision API:** Add image recognition and analysis features to your applications.
- **Twilio:** Integrate conversational AI into messaging and call-based apps.

5. Learning Resources

- **Online Courses:** Platforms like Coursera, Udemy, and edX offer AI development courses for all levels.
- **Documentation and Tutorials:** Official documentation for tools like TensorFlow and PyTorch provides in-depth guides.
- **AI Communities:** Engage with developers on forums like Stack Overflow and GitHub to learn and share knowledge.

Getting Started

If you're new to AI, start small:

- Choose a simple project, such as creating a chatbot using pre-built APIs.
- Familiarize yourself with user-friendly platforms like RunwayML.
- Gradually explore advanced tools and frameworks as your skills grow.

For seasoned developers, the key is to identify a real-world problem that AI can solve and create a solution that stands out. Build, test, iterate, and prepare to scale.

AI app development represents a limitless playground for innovation, creativity, and entrepreneurship. By harnessing these tools and insights, you can create applications that make a difference—and a profit.

Chapter 2: Selling AI-Driven Services

The demand for AI-driven services has skyrocketed as businesses across industries recognize the transformative potential of Artificial Intelligence. By offering AI consulting, automation, and optimization services, you can position yourself as a valuable partner in helping organizations achieve growth and efficiency.

Overview of AI-Driven Services

AI-driven services involve applying AI technologies to address specific business needs. These services can range from helping companies adopt AI to optimizing existing processes with AI solutions. Here are the most sought-after AI-driven services:

1. **AI Consulting**
   - **What It Involves:** Guiding businesses on how to implement AI to solve challenges and unlock opportunities.
   - **Examples:** Strategy development, technology selection, and feasibility studies.
2. **Process Automation**
   - **What It Involves:** Leveraging AI to automate repetitive tasks and workflows.
   - **Examples:** Robotic Process Automation (RPA), chatbots for customer service, and data entry automation.
3. **Data Analysis and Insights**
   - **What It Involves:** Using AI to analyze data and uncover actionable insights.
   - **Examples:** Predictive analytics, market trend analysis, and customer behavior modeling.

1. **Optimization Services**
   - **What It Involves:** Enhancing existing systems or processes with AI to improve efficiency and performance.
   - **Examples:** Supply chain optimization, dynamic pricing models, and personalized marketing campaigns.
2. **Custom AI Development**
   - **What It Involves:** Building tailored AI solutions to meet unique business needs.
   - **Examples:** Developing recommendation engines, fraud detection systems, or predictive maintenance tools.

How Businesses Are Leveraging AI Services for Growth

Companies are increasingly turning to AI-driven services to gain a competitive edge, improve customer experiences, and streamline operations. Here are a few ways businesses are benefiting:

1. **Enhanced Decision-Making**
   AI-powered analytics help businesses make data-driven decisions, reduce risks, and identify opportunities more effectively.
2. **Cost Savings Through Automation**
   Automating repetitive tasks allows businesses to cut costs, reduce errors, and free up human resources for more strategic activities.
3. **Improved Customer Experience**
   AI-powered chatbots, recommendation systems, and personalized content keep customers engaged and satisfied.
4. **Scalability and Innovation**
   AI services enable companies to scale operations seamlessly and innovate faster, adapting to changing market demands.

For example, a retail business using AI for dynamic pricing can optimize profits by adjusting prices in real-time based on demand and competition. Similarly, healthcare providers leveraging AI-driven diagnostics can offer faster, more accurate results, improving patient outcomes.

Tips for Marketing Your AI Expertise

If you want to succeed in selling AI-driven services, you need to demonstrate your value effectively. Here's how to do it:

1. **Identify Your Niche**
    - Focus on industries or services where you have expertise or see significant demand.
    - Tailor your offerings to specific problems, such as automating customer service for e-commerce or optimizing logistics for supply chain companies.
2. **Build a Strong Online Presence**
    - Create a professional website showcasing your services, case studies, and testimonials.
    - Share your knowledge through blogs, webinars, and social media posts to establish authority in the AI space.
3. **Leverage Freelance Platforms**
    - Platforms like Upwork, Fiverr, and Toptal are excellent for finding clients looking for AI services.
    - Highlight your AI skills, certifications, and successful projects in your profiles.

1. **Partner with Other Professionals**
    - Collaborate with software developers, data scientists, or industry experts to offer comprehensive solutions.
    - Build relationships with business consultants and agencies that can refer clients to you.
2. **Use Demonstrations and Prototypes**
    - Create simple demos or prototypes to showcase your capabilities. For example, show how a chatbot can handle customer inquiries or how an AI tool can optimize scheduling.
3. **Offer Free Workshops or Consultations**
    - Provide free initial consultations or workshops to educate potential clients about the benefits of AI and how your services can help.
4. **Stay Updated on Trends**
    - AI is evolving rapidly, so staying informed about the latest developments is crucial.
    - Use your knowledge of emerging trends to position yourself as a forward-thinking expert.

Getting Started

To begin selling AI-driven services:

- Assess your skills and determine which services align with your expertise.
- Research your target industries to understand their challenges and needs.
- Start with small projects to build your portfolio and gain experience.

Selling AI-driven services is not just about offering technical expertise—it's about solving problems, creating value, and building trust. By combining your AI skills with a strategic approach to marketing, you can unlock lucrative opportunities in this growing field.

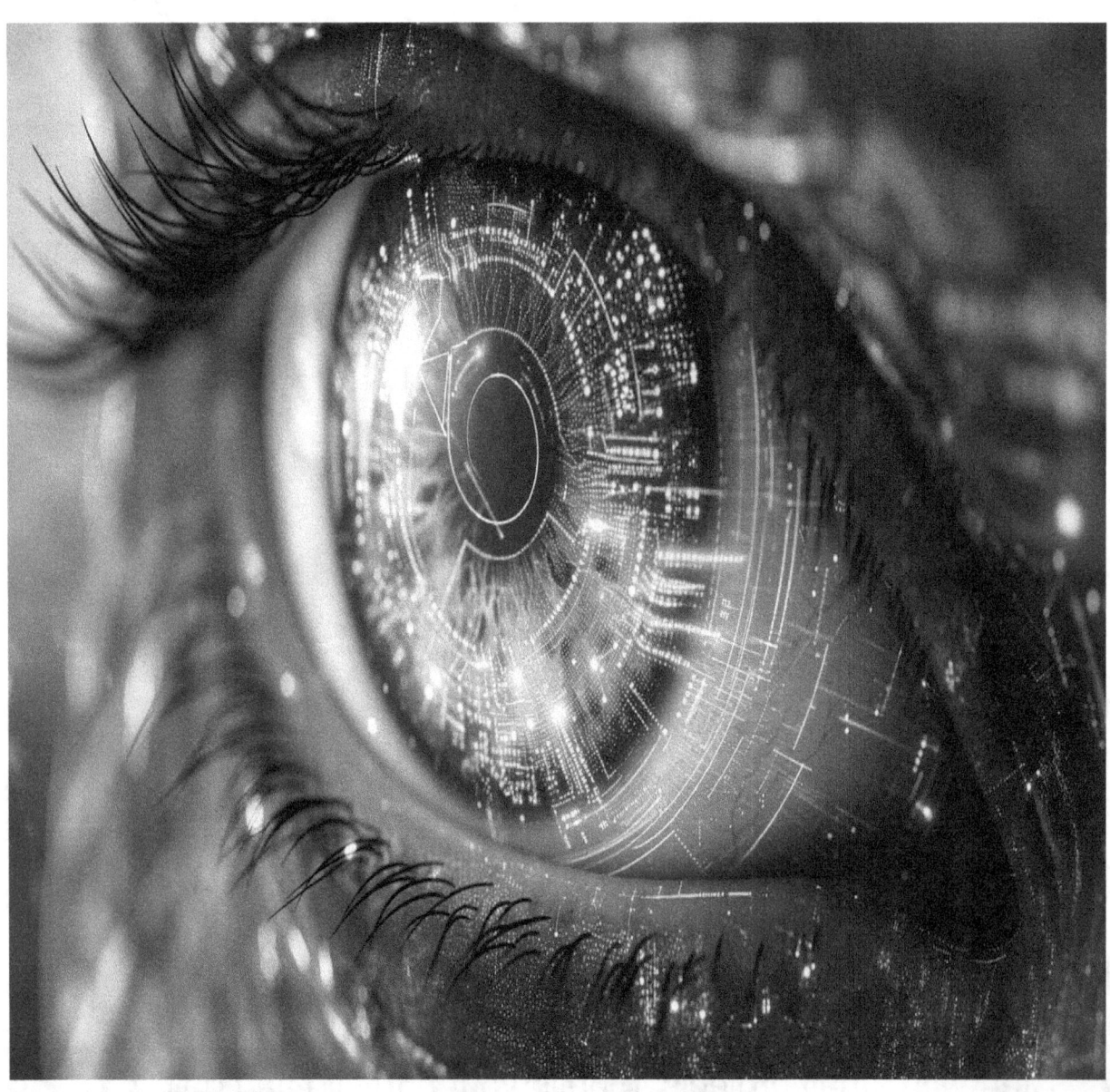

Chapter 3: Creating and Selling AI Content

Artificial Intelligence is revolutionizing content creation, enabling individuals and businesses to produce high-quality materials more efficiently than ever. From generating blog posts to crafting marketing campaigns, AI tools provide endless opportunities for creative expression and monetization. However, succeeding in this space also requires a solid understanding of legal and ethical considerations.

Using AI for Content Creation

AI tools are reshaping the way content is created by automating tasks and enhancing creativity. Here's how AI can assist with different types of content:

1. **Blog Posts and Articles**
   - **Tools to Use:**
     - ChatGPT or Jasper for writing engaging articles and SEO-optimized blog posts.
     - Grammarly or ProWritingAid for polishing language and grammar.
   - **Benefits:** Saves time, generates topic ideas, and drafts content that can be fine-tuned for publication.
2. **Videos and Visual Content**
   - **Tools to Use:**
     - Synthesia for creating AI-driven video presentations.
     - Pictory and RunwayML for video editing and animations.

- - - Canva or Adobe Firefly for designing stunning graphics with AI assistance.
  - **Benefits:** Enables creators to produce professional-quality videos, animations, and infographics quickly.
2. **Social Media Content**
   - **Tools to Use:**
     - Lumen5 for turning blog content into shareable videos.
     - Hootsuite Insights for AI-driven social media trends and scheduling.
   - **Benefits:** Generates captions, hashtags, and post ideas tailored to target audiences.
3. **Marketing Materials**
   - **Tools to Use:**
     - Copy.ai for creating compelling ad copy, email campaigns, and product descriptions.
     - HubSpot's AI tools for crafting customer-focused marketing strategies.
   - **Benefits:** Produces effective promotional materials to drive engagement and conversions.

Monetizing AI-Generated Content

AI-generated content can be monetized through various platforms and strategies. Here's how:

- **Blogging**
    - Start a blog and leverage AI to create regular, high-quality posts.
    - Monetization options include:
        - Display ads (Google AdSense, Mediavine).
        - Affiliate marketing by embedding product links.
        - Offering premium content or e-books.
- **YouTube and Video Platforms**
    - Use AI tools to create and edit videos for YouTube.
    - Popular video topics include tutorials, reviews, and storytelling.
    - Monetization options include:
        - Ad revenue through YouTube's Partner Program.
        - Sponsorships and brand deals.
        - Selling products or services directly to viewers.
- **Social Media and Influencer Marketing**
    - Use AI to generate consistent and engaging posts across platforms like Instagram, TikTok, and LinkedIn.
    - Monetization options include:
        - Sponsored content collaborations with brands.
        - Affiliate marketing and product endorsements.
        - Driving traffic to your own e-commerce or consulting services.
- **Selling Digital Products**
    - Use AI to create digital products like e-books, courses, or templates.
    - Platforms to sell: Gumroad, Teachable, or Shopify.

- **Freelancing and Consulting**
    - Offer AI-assisted content creation services to businesses and individuals.
    - Platforms like Upwork and Fiverr are ideal for finding clients.

Legal and Ethical Considerations in AI-Generated Content

While AI makes content creation easier, there are important legal and ethical guidelines to follow:

1. **Copyright Issues**
    - **Problem:** AI tools often use existing content to generate new material, raising concerns about copyright infringement.
    - **Solution:** Always verify the originality of your AI-generated content and avoid using tools that infringe on protected works.
2. **Plagiarism Concerns**
    - AI-generated text or visuals may unintentionally replicate existing work. Use plagiarism detection tools to ensure originality.
3. **Transparency and Disclosure**
    - If using AI-generated content in client projects or marketing materials, disclose its use to maintain trust.
4. **Quality Control**
    - AI-generated content may sometimes produce errors, biases, or inaccuracies. Always review and refine content before publishing.

1. **Data Privacy**
   - Be mindful of the data you input into AI tools, particularly if it includes sensitive or proprietary information.
2. **Ethical Use**
   - Avoid using AI for misleading or harmful purposes, such as creating fake reviews or manipulating audiences.

Getting Started

1. **Choose Your Niche**
   - Focus on a content type or topic you're passionate about (e.g., travel, technology, lifestyle).
2. **Select the Right Tools**
   - Experiment with different AI platforms to find those that best suit your needs.
3. **Plan Your Monetization Strategy**
   - Decide how you'll generate income: ads, sales, or services.
4. **Experiment and Iterate**
   - AI content creation is a process of trial and error. Test different approaches, analyze results, and refine your strategies.

By combining your creativity with the power of AI, you can create content that captivates audiences and generates income. With careful planning and ethical practices, you'll unlock the full potential of AI in the content economy.

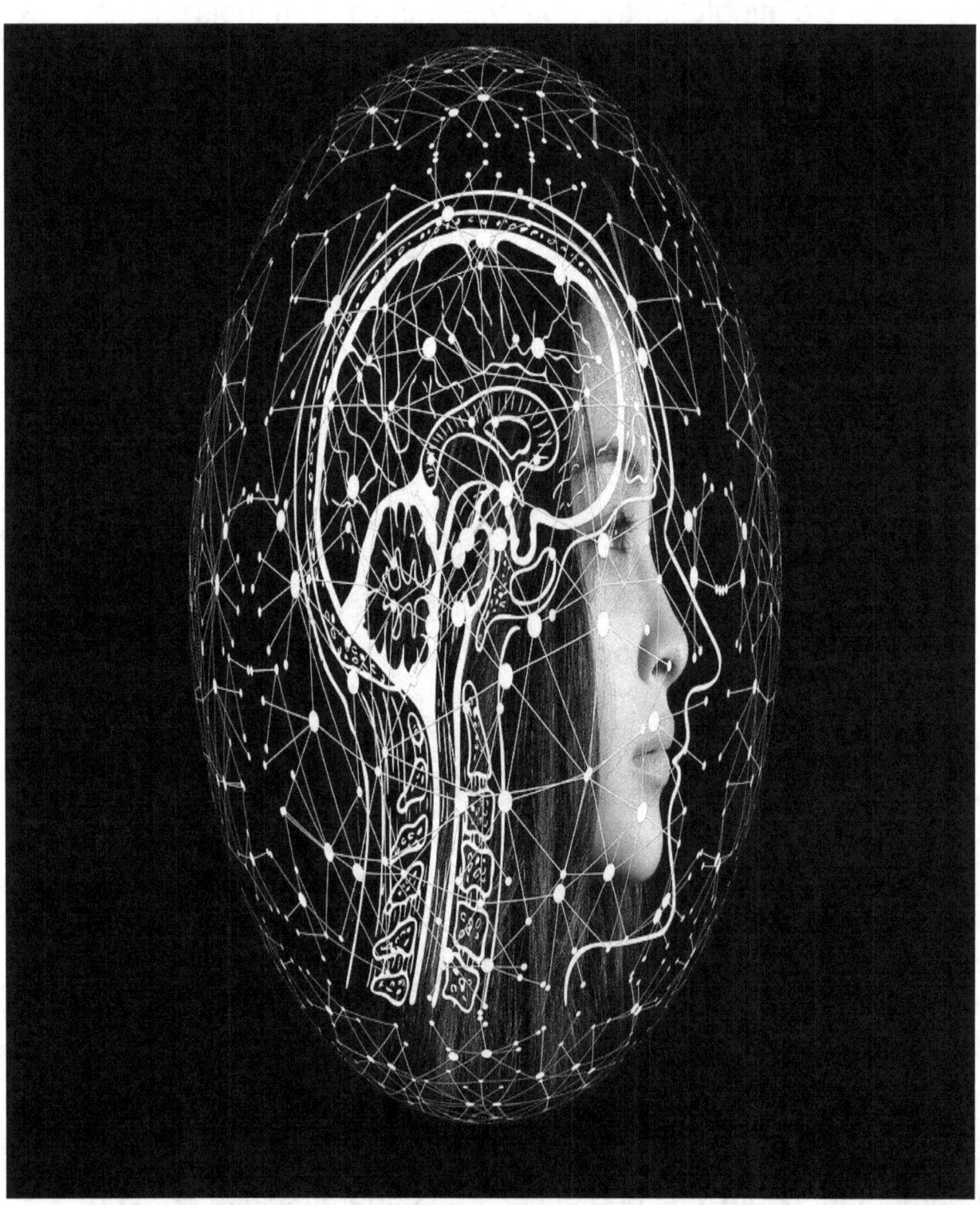

Chapter 4: Developing AI Courses and Educational Materials

As artificial intelligence continues to reshape industries, the demand for AI education is skyrocketing. Entrepreneurs and professionals have a golden opportunity to capitalize on this trend by creating and selling AI-related courses and educational materials. Whether you're an AI expert or simply someone with a passion for teaching, this chapter will guide you through the process of creating impactful educational content and reaching a global audience.

The Growing Demand for AI Education

AI is becoming integral to fields like business, healthcare, marketing, and software development. This has sparked a need for:

1. **Professional Training:** Companies are seeking ways to upskill their workforce with AI knowledge.
2. **Career Development:** Individuals aiming to future-proof their careers are investing in AI education.
3. **Beginner-Friendly Learning:** Many people are curious about AI but need beginner-level resources to get started.

Key Statistics:

- The global e-learning market is projected to reach $400 billion by 2026, with technology courses being among the top categories.
- AI and machine learning are consistently ranked as the most in-demand skills on platforms like LinkedIn.

This demand creates an ideal market for educators who can simplify complex AI topics for a diverse audience.

Creating AI Courses on Popular Platforms

Platforms like Udemy, Coursera, and Teachable have democratized the process of creating and distributing online courses. Here's how to get started:

1. **Choosing Your Niche**
    - Identify a specific topic within AI that aligns with your expertise. Examples include:
        - Introduction to AI for Beginners.
        - AI for Business Applications.
        - Machine Learning with Python.
        - AI Ethics and Responsible Use.
2. **Planning Your Course Content**
    - **Outline Your Modules:** Break down your course into manageable sections with clear learning objectives.
    - **Incorporate Practical Exercises:** Include hands-on activities like coding challenges, case studies, or real-world projects.
    - **Cater to Different Learning Styles:** Use a mix of videos, written materials, quizzes, and interactive elements.
3. **Creating High-Quality Content**
    - Use tools like Camtasia or OBS Studio for recording lectures and tutorials.
    - Leverage AI tools like ChatGPT or Grammarly to draft clear and concise scripts or instructional materials.

- Create visually engaging slides and infographics using tools like Canva or PowerPoint.
2. **Hosting Your Course**
    - **Udemy:** Ideal for beginner instructors with a large built-in audience.
    - **Coursera:** Great for more formal, credentialed courses, often in collaboration with institutions.
    - **Teachable/Kajabi:** Best for hosting courses on your own website, giving you full control over branding and pricing.

Structuring and Marketing Your AI Training Programs

1. **Structuring Your Course**
    - **Start with an Overview:** Provide an introduction that outlines the course's value and structure.
    - **Build Gradually:** Progress from foundational concepts to advanced applications.
    - **Include Assessments:** Use quizzes, assignments, or certification exams to reinforce learning.
    - **Offer Supplemental Materials:** Include downloadable resources like cheat sheets, datasets, or code templates.
2. **Marketing Your Course**
    - **Identify Your Target Audience:** Are you catering to beginners, professionals, or niche industries?
    - **Use Social Media:** Share course previews, testimonials, and educational content to attract students.
    - **Collaborate with Influencers:** Partner with industry professionals or influencers to promote your course.

- **Leverage SEO:** Optimize your course titles, descriptions, and content to rank high on search engines.
- **Offer Discounts:** Provide early-bird pricing or promotional discounts to drive initial enrollment.

2. **Maximizing Reach with AI Tools**
   - Use AI-driven platforms like Jasper or Writesonic to create compelling marketing copy.
   - Leverage tools like ChatGPT to draft email campaigns or blog posts promoting your course.
   - Utilize analytics platforms like Google Analytics or Hotjar to track engagement and optimize content.

Case Study: Success in AI Education

Example:

John Doe, an AI enthusiast, launched a beginner-level course on Udemy titled "AI for Business Leaders." His course featured easy-to-understand video lectures, real-world examples, and interactive exercises. By targeting professionals with limited technical backgrounds, John reached over 10,000 students in the first year, earning $100,000 in revenue.

Expanding Your Offerings

1. **Webinars and Live Workshops:** Host live sessions to engage directly with learners.
2. **Subscription Models:** Offer ongoing learning through monthly memberships or access to a library of resources.

1. **Corporate Training Programs:** Partner with businesses to provide tailored AI education for their teams.
2. **Books and eBooks:** Create supplemental materials to complement your courses and expand your reach.

By combining your expertise with the tools and strategies outlined in this chapter, you can create and market AI courses that meet the needs of learners worldwide. The key to success lies in simplifying complex concepts, providing real-world value, and continuously refining your content based on learner feedback.

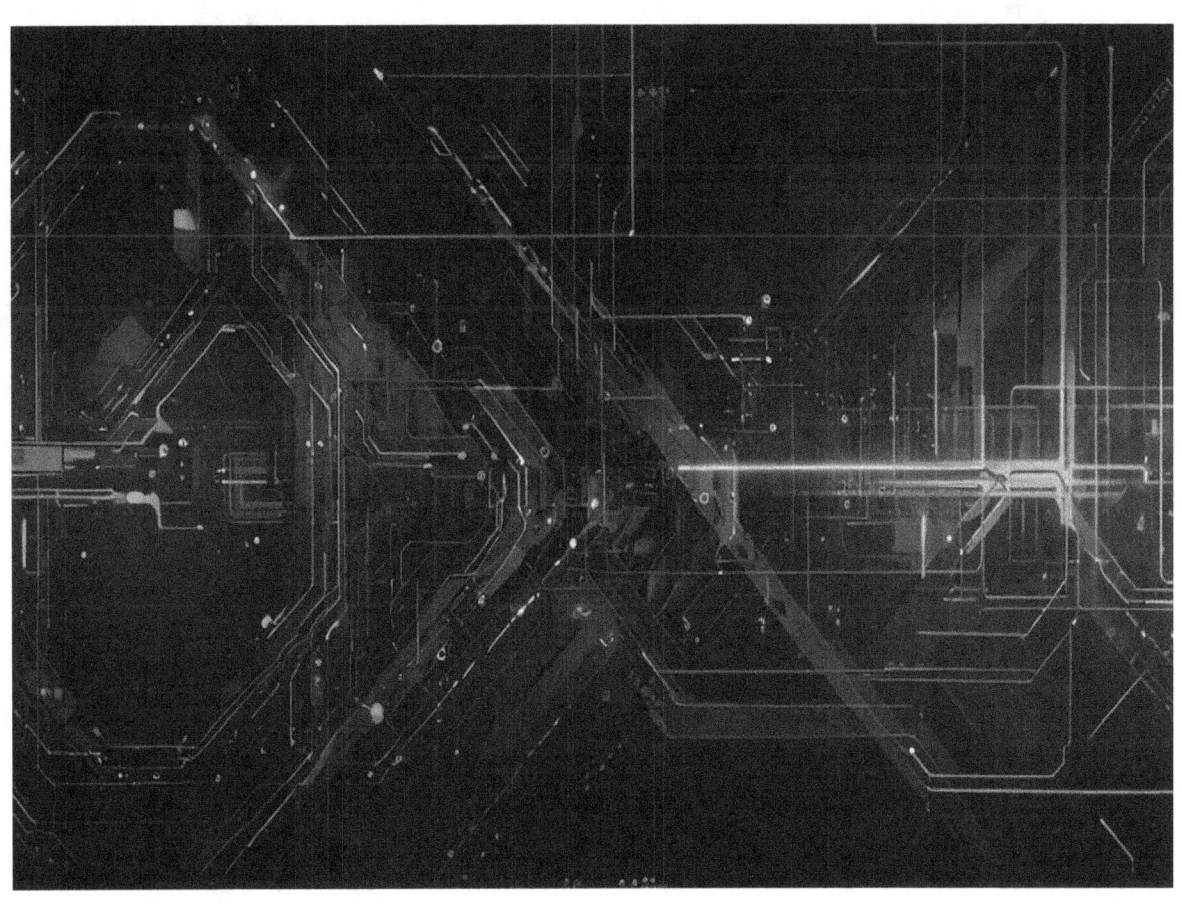

Chapter 5: Investing in AI Startups and Technologies

Artificial intelligence is a frontier with immense growth potential, making it a hotbed for investment opportunities. This chapter explores how individuals and organizations can participate in the AI revolution through strategic investments. By understanding the landscape, evaluating startups effectively, and managing risks, you can position yourself for success in this dynamic sector.

Overview of the AI Investment Landscape

1. **The Current AI Boom**
   - AI technologies are being integrated across industries like healthcare, finance, retail, and transportation.
   - Key AI-driven innovations include natural language processing (NLP), autonomous systems, predictive analytics, and generative AI.
   - The global AI market is expected to grow at a compound annual growth rate (CAGR) of 35.6%, reaching over $500 billion by 2028.
2. **Types of AI Investments**
   - **Seed Investments:** Supporting early-stage startups with innovative ideas but limited track records.
   - **Series Investments:** Funding more mature startups to scale their operations.
   - **Public Markets:** Investing in AI-focused stocks or ETFs.
   - **Private Equity and Venture Capital:** Participating in larger investment rounds with established firms.

- **Key Players in the AI Ecosystem**
  - **Startups:** Innovators building cutting-edge solutions.
  - **Big Tech Companies:** Firms like Google, Microsoft, and Amazon are investing billions in AI research and acquisitions.
  - **Research Institutions:** Universities and labs contributing foundational advancements.

How to Identify and Evaluate Promising AI Startups

Investing in AI startups requires a careful balance of vision and due diligence. Here's a roadmap:

1. **Spotting Trends and Niches**
   - Identify sectors where AI is creating disruption (e.g., autonomous vehicles, personalized medicine).
   - Look for startups addressing critical problems with scalable solutions.
2. **Evaluating the Team**
   - Assess the founders' backgrounds, technical expertise, and industry connections.
   - Strong teams often include both technical AI experts and savvy business leaders.
3. **Analyzing the Product**
   - Determine if the AI solution is innovative or offers a significant improvement over existing technologies.
   - Understand the underlying technology (e.g., algorithms, datasets, models) and its defensibility.

- **Examining the Market Potential**
    - Assess the total addressable market (TAM) and the startup's positioning.
    - Look for clear paths to revenue, such as subscription models, licensing, or service agreements.
- **Checking Financial Health**
    - Review the startup's funding history, burn rate, and revenue projections.
    - Analyze key financial metrics to ensure sustainable growth.
- **Evaluating Partnerships and Clients**
    - Startups with partnerships in place (e.g., with corporations or academic institutions) may have a higher chance of success.
    - Existing clients demonstrate market validation and demand.

Risks and Rewards of Investing in AI

Investing in AI offers tremendous potential but comes with inherent challenges.

1. **Potential Rewards**
    - **High Returns:** Successful startups can deliver exponential gains.
    - **Portfolio Diversification:** AI investments offer exposure to cutting-edge industries.
    - **Positive Impact:** Support innovations that can transform industries and solve global problems.

- **Key Risks**
  - **Technological Uncertainty:** Rapid advancements can render technologies obsolete.
  - **Regulatory Challenges:** AI faces scrutiny regarding privacy, bias, and ethical concerns.
  - **Market Competition:** Startups must compete with both peers and established tech giants.
  - **Execution Risks:** Even strong ideas can falter due to poor execution or lack of resources.
- **Risk Mitigation Strategies**
  - Diversify investments across multiple AI startups and sectors.
  - Focus on startups with defensible technology and clear market validation.
  - Engage with industry experts and advisors for informed decision-making.

Case Studies: Success and Lessons in AI Investment

1. **Success Story: OpenAI**
   - Early investments in OpenAI laid the groundwork for its GPT models, now widely adopted and generating significant revenue through APIs and licensing.
2. **Learning from Challenges**
   - Many AI startups fail to scale due to unrealistic goals or over-reliance on untested technology. Learning from such cases can sharpen your evaluation skills.

Getting Started as an AI Investor

1. **Building Your Network**
   - Join AI-focused investment groups, forums, or accelerators.
   - Attend conferences and pitch events to connect with promising startups.
2. **Exploring Investment Platforms**
   - **AngelList:** Discover early-stage AI startups seeking funding.
   - **Equity Crowdfunding:** Participate in platforms like SeedInvest or Republic.
   - **Venture Capital Funds:** Partner with VC firms specializing in AI investments.
3. **Continual Learning**
   - Stay updated on AI trends through blogs, podcasts, and industry reports.
   - Take courses on AI and investment strategies to refine your expertise.

- By understanding the nuances of the AI investment landscape and applying strategic evaluation methods, you can unlock the potential of this transformative sector. Remember, successful investments require not just capital but also foresight, patience, and a commitment to continuous learning.

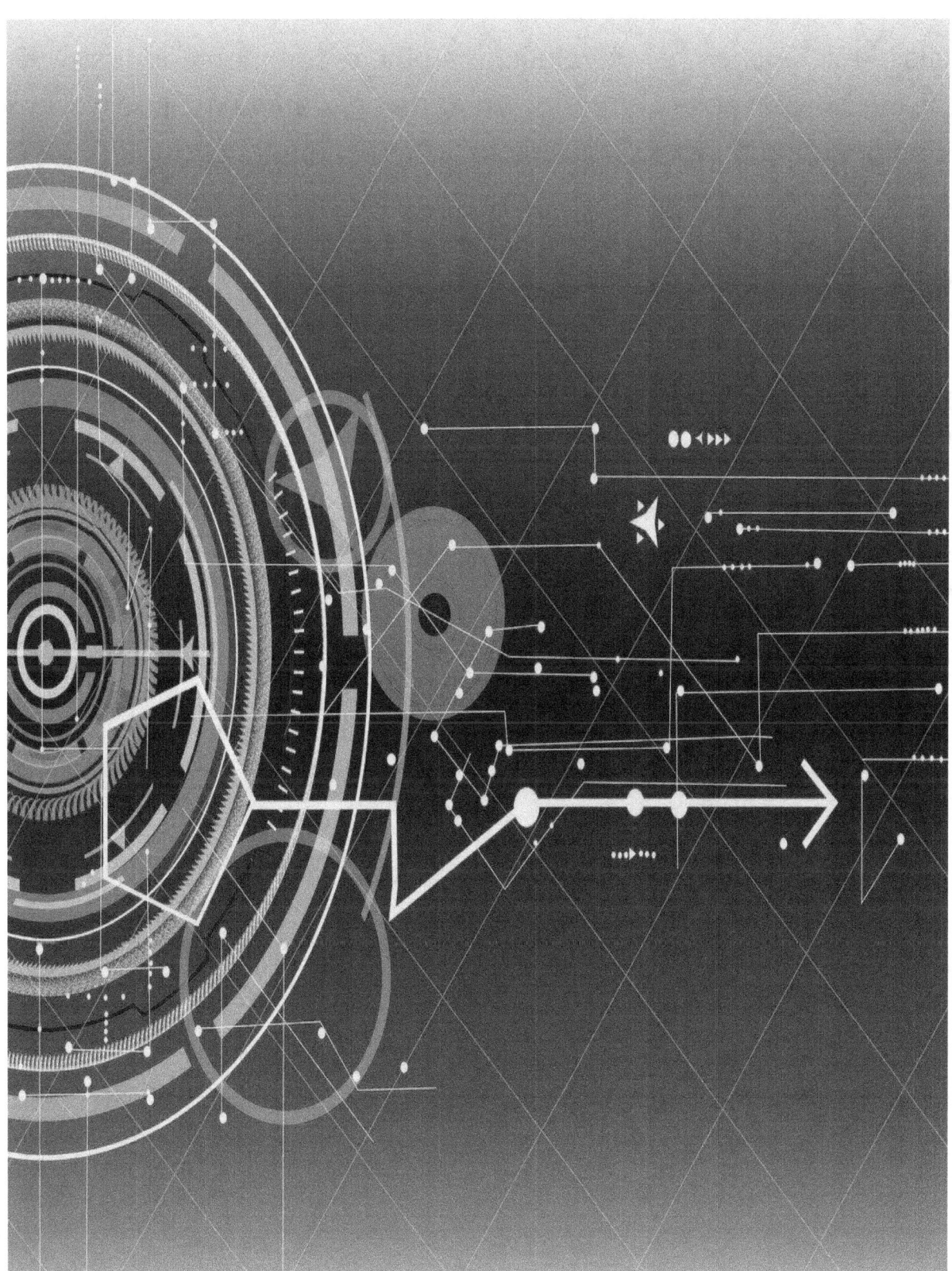

Chapter 6: Leveraging AI for E-Commerce

Artificial Intelligence has revolutionized the e-commerce industry, enabling businesses to enhance customer experiences, streamline operations, and boost sales. This chapter explores how entrepreneurs and businesses can integrate AI into their online stores to stay competitive and maximize profits.

Using AI for Product Recommendations, Customer Service, and Inventory Management

AI provides powerful tools to optimize various aspects of e-commerce, ensuring efficiency and personalization.

1. **Product Recommendations**
    - **Personalized Recommendations:** AI analyzes customer behavior and preferences to suggest products tailored to individual tastes.
    - **Upselling and Cross-Selling:** Algorithms identify complementary products, increasing average order values.
    - **Dynamic Suggestions:** Real-time analytics adapt recommendations based on trends and seasonal demands.
2. *Example*: Amazon's recommendation engine, powered by machine learning, accounts for up to 35% of its sales.
3. **Customer Service**
    - **AI Chatbots:** Offer instant responses to customer queries, reducing wait times and enhancing satisfaction.

- - **Sentiment Analysis:** AI detects customer emotions and adjusts responses to improve interactions.
  - **Automated Responses:** Common issues like order tracking and refunds can be resolved without human intervention.
- *Example*: Shopify's "Kit" helps store owners communicate with customers and automate marketing efforts.
- **Inventory Management**
  - **Demand Forecasting:** AI predicts product demand, helping businesses avoid overstocking or stockouts.
  - **Smart Reordering:** Automates restocking processes based on sales data and trends.
  - **Warehouse Optimization:** AI enhances supply chain logistics, reducing operational costs.
- *Example*: Zara uses AI-driven inventory systems to streamline production and reduce waste.

Tools and Platforms to Integrate AI into Your Online Store

Integrating AI into e-commerce is easier than ever, thanks to a range of accessible tools and platforms.

1. **AI-Powered Tools for Small Businesses**
   - **Google Cloud AI:** Offers tools for personalized recommendations and demand forecasting.
   - **Zendesk AI Chatbot:** Simplifies customer service with pre-trained conversational agents.
   - **Inventory Planner:** Uses AI to analyze sales trends and optimize inventory.

1. **AI Integration Platforms**
    - **Shopify with AI Apps:** Plugins like Bold Brain and ReConvert use AI to drive sales.
    - **BigCommerce:** Offers AI-enhanced features like personalized marketing and analytics.
    - **WooCommerce Extensions:** AI-powered tools like "WooCommerce Smart Coupons" for customized offers.
2. **Enterprise-Grade Solutions**
    - **Salesforce Einstein:** AI for personalized marketing, sales predictions, and customer engagement.
    - **SAP AI for E-Commerce:** Helps large-scale businesses with advanced demand forecasting and customer insights.
    - **IBM Watson Commerce:** Offers solutions for personalized shopping experiences and customer analytics.

Real-World Case Studies of AI in E-Commerce

1. **Amazon: The Pioneer of AI in E-Commerce**
    - *AI Innovations*: Product recommendations, automated warehouses, and dynamic pricing.
    - *Impact*: AI-driven personalization and logistics efficiency have positioned Amazon as a market leader.
2. **Stitch Fix: Personalized Shopping at Scale**
    - *AI Applications*: Uses machine learning to curate clothing recommendations for individual customers.
    - *Outcome*: Increased customer satisfaction and retention due to hyper-personalized experiences.

1. **Sephora: AI-Driven Beauty Retail**
   - *AI Features*: Virtual assistants like the "Sephora Virtual Artist" help customers visualize products.
   - *Result*: Higher conversion rates and an enhanced online shopping experience.
2. **Alibaba: Smart Logistics and Search**
   - *AI Solutions*: Autonomous logistics systems and natural language processing for search optimization.
   - *Result*: Faster delivery times and a seamless shopping experience for millions of users.

Steps to Start Leveraging AI for Your E-Commerce Store

1. **Identify Key Areas for Improvement**
   - Determine whether customer service, recommendations, or inventory management needs enhancement.
2. **Choose the Right Tools**
   - Start with accessible platforms that align with your store's size and budget.
3. **Implement Gradually**
   - Roll out AI solutions in phases, testing their impact on customer satisfaction and sales.
4. **Monitor and Optimize**
   - Use analytics to evaluate AI's performance and tweak systems as needed.

- By leveraging AI, you can transform your e-commerce business into a customer-centric and efficient operation. As AI technology continues to advance, staying informed and adaptable will ensure long-term success in this highly competitive industry.

Chapter 7: Monetizing AI-Generated Art and Media

Artificial Intelligence has unlocked new opportunities in creative industries, allowing individuals and businesses to generate and sell unique art, music, and multimedia content. This chapter dives into the tools, platforms, and strategies for monetizing AI-generated creations while addressing the ethical and legal considerations involved.

Exploring AI Tools for Art, Music, and Multimedia Creation

AI tools enable creators to produce high-quality art and media efficiently, often blurring the line between human and machine creativity.

1. **AI for Visual Art**
   - **Art Generators:** Tools like DALL-E, Stable Diffusion, and DeepArt create stunning visuals from text prompts or style transfers.
   - **Customization:** Artists can adjust styles, colors, and details to personalize their creations.
2. *Example*: An AI-generated painting sold at auction for over $400,000, showcasing the demand for such works.
3. **AI for Music**
   - **Music Composition:** Platforms like AIVA and Amper Music allow users to create original soundtracks or beats in minutes.
   - **Mixing and Mastering:** AI tools like LANDR automate professional-quality music production.

1. *Example*: Musicians use AI-generated tracks as royalty-free background music for videos and commercials.
2. **AI for Video and Multimedia**
    - **Video Editing:** Tools like Runway and Pictory AI enable the creation of dynamic video content with minimal effort.
    - **Animation and Effects:** Software like DeepMotion and Kaiber adds lifelike animations to static images or videos.
3. *Example*: Social media influencers use AI to enhance video production, increasing engagement.

Platforms for Selling AI-Generated Creative Works

Monetizing AI-generated art and media involves leveraging platforms designed for creators and marketplaces.

1. **Digital Art Marketplaces**
    - **Etsy and Redbubble:** Perfect for selling prints, digital downloads, or merchandise featuring AI-generated art.
    - **ArtStation and DeviantArt:** Great for showcasing and selling AI-created artworks to a global audience.
2. **NFT Platforms**
    - **OpenSea and Rarible:** Ideal for turning AI art into non-fungible tokens (NFTs) and selling them as digital assets.
    - **Foundation and SuperRare:** Focus on high-quality, exclusive AI-generated artworks.

1. **Music and Sound Marketplaces**
   - **AudioJungle and Pond5:** Allow creators to sell AI-generated music and sound effects for commercial use.
   - **Spotify and SoundCloud:** Distribute AI-created tracks to a wider audience, earning royalties through streaming.
2. **Video Content Platforms**
   - **YouTube and TikTok:** Monetize AI-enhanced or entirely AI-created videos through ads, sponsorships, and merchandise.
   - **Stock Video Sites:** Upload AI-generated clips to platforms like Shutterstock and Adobe Stock for passive income.

Addressing Copyright and Originality Concerns

As AI-generated content grows in popularity, legal and ethical questions about ownership and originality arise.

1. **Copyright Challenges**
   - **Who Owns AI Creations?** In many jurisdictions, copyright for AI-generated works may not automatically belong to the user.
   - **Attribution:** Ensure compliance with the terms of AI tools, which may require acknowledgment of the software's role.
2. **Avoiding Plagiarism**
   - **Dataset Transparency:** Check if the AI tool used relies on datasets with copyrighted materials to avoid infringement claims.
   - **Modifications:** Make substantial alterations to AI-generated works to increase originality and creativity.

- **Ethical Considerations**
  - **Authenticity:** Clearly disclose whether a piece is AI-generated to maintain transparency with buyers.
  - **Bias and Representation:** Be mindful of biases in AI-generated content, particularly when creating works for diverse audiences.

Real-World Examples of AI-Generated Media Monetization

1. **AI-Generated NFTs**
   - *Case Study*: An artist used GANs (Generative Adversarial Networks) to create unique digital paintings, selling them for millions as NFTs.
2. **AI in Stock Media**
   - *Case Study*: Freelancers sell AI-generated stock images and videos to supplement income, capitalizing on high demand for content.
3. **AI-Enhanced Music**
   - *Case Study*: A small business uses AI-generated soundtracks for YouTube ads, avoiding costly licensing fees while maintaining quality.

Steps to Start Monetizing AI-Generated Art and Media

1. **Choose Your Niche**
   - Decide whether to focus on visual art, music, video, or a combination of media types.

- **Master the Tools**
  - Experiment with leading AI tools to produce professional-quality outputs.
- **Select Your Platform**
  - Pick marketplaces that align with your chosen medium and audience.
- **Market Your Creations**
  - Use social media, email marketing, and partnerships to promote your work.
- **Stay Updated**
  - Keep up with legal updates and technological advancements to remain competitive.

AI has democratized access to creative tools, empowering individuals to explore and profit from their artistic pursuits. By addressing legal and ethical considerations and leveraging the right platforms, you can build a successful business in the burgeoning AI-driven creative industry.

Chapter 8: Developing Niche AI Tools

Artificial Intelligence has the potential to revolutionize virtually every industry, and identifying niche markets for AI tools is a great way to capitalize on underserved areas. This chapter explores how entrepreneurs can develop AI tools for specific niches, the success stories of such tools, and the best strategies for monetization.

Identifying Underserved Niches and Developing AI Solutions

The first step in developing a successful niche AI tool is identifying gaps in the market where AI can offer valuable solutions.

1. **Conduct Market Research**
    - **Look for Pain Points:** Identify industries or sectors where current tools are inadequate, outdated, or nonexistent.
    - **Analyze Trends:** Study emerging trends in AI, such as automation, predictive analytics, and natural language processing, and find ways to apply them to niche markets.
    - **Survey Potential Users:** Engage with professionals in niche fields to understand their specific challenges and needs that AI could address.
2. **AI in Specialized Industries**
    - **Healthcare:** AI-powered tools for niche medical fields, such as AI for rare disease diagnosis or predictive tools for patient care.

- **Legal Tech:** Automating routine legal tasks like document review, contract analysis, and case law research for smaller law firms.
- **Agriculture:** AI solutions for crop management, pest detection, or precision farming tailored to smaller or organic farms.
- **Elderly Care:** AI tools for senior citizen safety, health tracking, and companionship, designed specifically for the aging population.

2. **Innovating Existing Tools for Niche Markets**
   - **Customizing General AI Tools:** Tailor existing AI solutions to meet the unique needs of a specific industry.
   - **New Applications:** Apply AI techniques (such as machine learning and natural language processing) in unexpected ways for small, specialized industries.

Case Studies of Niche AI Tool Success Stories

Exploring successful examples of niche AI tools can provide inspiration and demonstrate the potential of focused AI solutions.

1. **Zocdoc – AI for Healthcare Scheduling**
   - **Niche:** Health tech, particularly for booking medical appointments.
   - **Solution:** Zocdoc created an AI-powered platform that enables patients to easily find doctors, book appointments, and manage healthcare visits.

- **Success:** By addressing the complexity of healthcare scheduling, Zocdoc has become a widely used tool in the U.S., growing its user base significantly in a relatively underserved niche.
2. **RPA in the Legal Industry – Ross Intelligence**
    - **Niche:** Legal research and AI-driven document review.
    - **Solution:** Ross Intelligence developed an AI tool that helps lawyers conduct legal research more efficiently by analyzing large volumes of case law.
    - **Success:** Ross Intelligence provided a major productivity boost for small law firms, allowing them to compete with larger firms and saving hours of manual research.
3. **Plantix – AI for Agriculture**
    - **Niche:** Agriculture and crop management.
    - **Solution:** Plantix created an AI-powered tool for identifying plant diseases, pests, and nutrient deficiencies from photos taken by users.
    - **Success:** The app gained rapid popularity, especially in developing markets, helping farmers reduce crop losses and increase yields by using AI for proactive management.

How to Monetize Through Subscriptions or One-Time Sales

Once you've developed a niche AI tool, monetizing it effectively is key to turning it into a profitable business.

1. **Subscription-Based Monetization**
   - **SaaS Model (Software as a Service):** Offer your AI tool on a subscription basis, providing continuous updates and support. This model ensures recurring revenue, which is valuable for long-term sustainability.
     - *Example*: Many AI tools in the legal and healthcare fields follow a SaaS model, charging monthly or annual fees for access to the platform.
   - **Freemium Model:** Offer a basic version of your AI tool for free, while charging for premium features, such as advanced analytics, additional storage, or more frequent updates.
     - *Example*: Tools like Grammarly and Zoom offer free basic versions with the option to upgrade for advanced capabilities.
2. **One-Time Sales**
   - **Single License Sales:** Sell the AI tool for a one-time fee, providing lifetime access to the product. This is a good model if your tool addresses a very specific niche need that doesn't require constant updates or features.
     - *Example*: A one-time sale model works well for smaller AI tools in industries like photography (e.g., AI-based photo enhancement software) or personal finance (e.g., AI budgeting tools).
   - **White-Labeling or Custom Solutions:** Offer your AI tool as a white-label product, which businesses can brand and resell under their own name. You can charge a one-time fee for the initial software purchase or create a licensing agreement for ongoing use.

- *Example*: Custom AI tools built for specific business operations (e.g., sales tracking or predictive analytics) are often white-labeled for use in a variety of industries.

2. **Licensing**
   - **Data Licensing:** If your AI tool leverages proprietary datasets or algorithms, you can license this data to other companies that may want to use it for their own purposes.
     - *Example*: An AI tool that offers specialized predictive analytics for the finance industry could license its predictive models to banks or investment firms.
   - **Algorithm Licensing:** License your AI model's underlying algorithm or software to other developers who want to build upon or integrate it into their own products.

Steps to Start Developing Niche AI Tools

1. **Research and Identify a Niche**
   - Study various industries and consult with potential users to identify specific pain points that could be addressed with AI.
2. **Build a Prototype or MVP (Minimum Viable Product)**
   - Develop a simple version of your AI tool that solves the core problem. Focus on user feedback to improve the product.

1. **Choose Your Monetization Strategy**
   - Decide whether a subscription, one-time sale, or licensing model works best for your target audience and the type of tool you're offering.
2. **Market Your AI Tool**
   - Use targeted marketing strategies, such as content marketing, partnerships with industry influencers, and paid advertising, to reach potential users.
3. **Optimize and Scale**
   - Continuously improve your tool based on user feedback, industry trends, and new advancements in AI to maintain competitiveness in your niche market.

By identifying underserved niches and developing AI solutions that address specific needs, you can carve out a profitable space in the AI landscape. Monetizing these tools through subscription models, one-time sales, or licensing agreements allows you to create a sustainable and scalable business.

Chapter 9: Using AI for Stock Market Analysis and Trading

The world of finance has seen a significant transformation with the introduction of Artificial Intelligence (AI) in stock market analysis and trading. AI-powered tools allow traders and investors to make more informed, faster decisions based on complex data patterns, enhancing the potential for profitability. However, there are both risks and opportunities when using AI in financial markets, and understanding these is essential for anyone looking to harness this technology. This chapter explores the fundamentals of AI in trading, popular tools, and strategies for success.

Introduction to AI in Financial Markets

1. **AI's Role in Stock Market Analysis**
    - **Data Processing and Analysis**: AI can process vast amounts of historical and real-time market data far more efficiently than human analysts. Machine learning algorithms identify patterns, trends, and correlations that may be invisible to traditional analysis.
    - **Predictive Modeling**: AI-powered tools use machine learning models to predict future price movements, volatility, and trends by analyzing historical data and identifying patterns in the stock market.
    - **Risk Assessment and Portfolio Management**: AI can analyze the risk profiles of different stocks and assets, optimize portfolios based on risk-return preferences, and provide suggestions for diversification.

1. **Key Benefits of AI in Trading**
   - **Speed and Efficiency**: AI systems can make decisions within milliseconds, trading far quicker than human traders.
   - **Emotionless Trading**: Unlike human traders, AI algorithms don't experience emotions such as fear or greed, which can lead to more rational trading decisions.
   - **Improved Accuracy**: Machine learning models improve over time as they are exposed to more data, enhancing their predictive power and decision-making.

Popular AI-Powered Trading Platforms and Tools

1. **Robo-Advisors**
   - **Overview**: Robo-advisors are AI-powered platforms that provide automated, algorithm-driven financial planning services with little to no human intervention. They create personalized investment portfolios based on individual preferences and financial goals.
   - **Popular Platforms**:
     - *Betterment*: One of the leading robo-advisors, it offers automated investment advice based on AI models and user risk preferences.
     - *Wealthfront*: Offers similar services with an emphasis on tax optimization and portfolio management.
2. **AI Trading Bots**
   - **Overview**: AI trading bots use machine learning to trade on your behalf, executing buy and sell orders based on

- predetermined parameters or real-time data analysis. These bots can trade in various asset classes, including stocks, forex, and cryptocurrencies.
- **Popular Bots**:
  - *3Commas*: Known for its cryptocurrency trading bots, 3Commas uses AI to make buy/sell decisions based on market data.
  - *TradeSanta*: Another bot offering automation for both crypto and stock trading, integrating with major platforms like Binance and Kraken.

2. **Quantitative Trading Platforms**
   - **Overview**: Quantitative trading platforms use AI models and sophisticated algorithms to perform high-frequency trading (HFT) and quantitative analysis. These platforms allow for backtesting strategies and implementing algorithmic trading in real-time.
   - **Popular Platforms**:
     - *QuantConnect*: An open-source platform for developing, testing, and executing algorithmic trading strategies using AI models.
     - *MetaTrader*: A widely used platform with AI capabilities for algorithmic trading, commonly used in forex markets.

3. **AI-Powered Stock Analysis Tools**
   - **Overview**: AI tools can be used to analyze stock prices, financial statements, and macroeconomic data to inform trading decisions. They can provide deep insights through sentiment analysis, news mining, and social media trends.

- **Popular Tools**:
    - *Kavout*: An AI-powered stock ranking system that uses deep learning to evaluate and rank stocks based on various factors, including financial reports, news sentiment, and price trends.
    - *Trade Ideas*: Offers AI-driven strategies for stock picking, scanning, and real-time alerts based on predictive algorithms.

Risks and Strategies for Using AI in Trading

2. **Risks of Using AI in Trading**
    - **Overfitting**: AI models can become overly complex and "overfit" to historical data, meaning they perform well in past market conditions but fail in new or unforeseen scenarios.
    - **Market Volatility**: AI systems are designed to analyze historical trends, but they may struggle in volatile markets or when faced with unprecedented events (e.g., financial crises, black swan events).
    - **Data Dependency**: AI systems are only as good as the data fed into them. If data quality is poor or biased, AI predictions can be inaccurate.
    - **Algorithmic Trading Risks**: High-frequency trading bots and AI algorithms can lead to flash crashes or market disruptions if they make erroneous trades due to bugs, faulty data, or incorrect assumptions.

- **Regulatory and Ethical Issues**: Regulatory bodies may impose restrictions on the use of AI in financial markets, particularly in areas such as algorithmic trading, data privacy, and transparency.
- **Strategies for Using AI in Trading**
    - **Diversify Strategies**: Don't rely solely on one AI tool or trading strategy. Use a combination of approaches, such as a blend of fundamental analysis, technical indicators, and machine learning models, to mitigate risks.
    - **Use Stop-Losses and Risk Management**: Even with AI, it's crucial to use proper risk management techniques like stop-loss orders to limit potential losses. Implement rules that prevent AI bots from making trades in volatile market conditions or during unexpected events.
    - **Regular Backtesting**: Continuously backtest your AI-driven strategies using historical data to ensure that they remain profitable and adapt to new market conditions.
    - **Monitor AI Systems Regularly**: Though AI can operate independently, it's important to monitor its performance to ensure that it continues to function as expected. Keep an eye on the trades it executes and ensure that any anomalies are addressed promptly.
    - **Stay Informed**: Stay updated on AI developments and financial market news. AI tools can process information faster, but they still need human insight into global trends and market psychology.

- **Conclusion: The Future of AI in Stock Market Analysis and Trading**
- AI has the potential to revolutionize stock market analysis and trading, making it more accessible, efficient, and data-driven. As AI tools and algorithms continue to improve, traders and investors will have an increasing ability to analyze vast amounts of data and predict market movements with greater accuracy. However, the risks associated with using AI, such as overfitting and volatility, must be managed carefully. By understanding the right tools, strategies, and risks, individuals and institutions can leverage AI to gain an edge in the stock market.

Chapter 10: Offering AI Automation for Businesses

AI automation is transforming industries by enabling businesses to streamline operations, enhance productivity, and reduce costs. From automating routine tasks to implementing complex AI-driven solutions, businesses across all sectors are leveraging AI to improve efficiency. In this chapter, we will explore how AI can automate various business processes, the steps to develop and sell AI-powered automation solutions, and how to build lasting relationships with clients.

How AI Can Streamline Operations in Various Industries

Manufacturing and Supply Chain

Robotics and AI Integration: AI-powered robots can handle repetitive tasks like assembly, packaging, and quality control, improving production speed and reducing human error.

Predictive Maintenance: AI can predict when machines or equipment are likely to fail, allowing businesses to perform maintenance proactively, reducing downtime and extending the life of assets.

Supply Chain Optimization: AI-driven tools can forecast demand, manage inventory, and optimize logistics, ensuring that products are delivered on time and with minimal waste.

Customer Service and Support

AI Chatbots: AI chatbots can provide instant support to customers, answering frequently asked questions, assisting with troubleshooting, and handling basic inquiries, freeing up human agents for more complex tasks.

Sentiment Analysis: AI can analyze customer feedback and social media sentiment to provide businesses with valuable insights about customer satisfaction and areas for improvement.

Automated Ticketing Systems: AI systems can prioritize and route customer service requests, ensuring that urgent issues are addressed quickly and efficiently.

Sales and Marketing

Lead Generation and Nurturing: AI can analyze data to identify potential leads, score them based on likelihood to convert, and automate follow-up tasks, allowing sales teams to focus on high-priority prospects.

Personalized Marketing Campaigns: AI tools can segment customer data and create personalized content and offers, maximizing the effectiveness of email campaigns, advertisements, and social media promotions.

Predictive Analytics for Sales: AI models can predict future sales trends based on historical data, helping businesses plan inventory, staffing, and marketing efforts more accurately.

Human Resources and Recruitment

- Automated Recruitment: AI can screen resumes, match candidates to job descriptions, and schedule interviews, significantly reducing the time and effort required in the hiring process.

- Employee Performance Monitoring: AI tools can track employee performance, analyze productivity metrics, and identify areas for improvement, helping HR departments make more data-driven decisions.

- Employee Retention: AI can analyze employee behavior patterns and identify at-risk employees, enabling HR teams to intervene early and prevent turnover.

Finance and Accounting

- Automated Invoicing and Payments: AI can automate invoicing, reconciliation, and payments, reducing administrative overhead and minimizing errors.

- Fraud Detection: AI algorithms can monitor transactions in real-time and flag any potentially fraudulent activities, helping businesses reduce financial risks.

- Financial Forecasting: AI-powered tools can predict cash flow trends, help businesses set budgets, and optimize financial strategies based on data analysis.

- Developing and Selling AI-Powered Automation Solution

Identifying Business Needs

- Understand Pain Points: Start by identifying common operational inefficiencies within industries you plan to serve. Conduct surveys, interviews, and research to understand the specific challenges that businesses face.

- Focus on High-Impact Areas: Automating core business functions such as customer service, marketing, or inventory management can have a high return on investment (ROI). Prioritize solutions that will drive cost savings or revenue growth for your clients.

- Tailor Solutions to Industry Needs: Customize AI automation solutions to the specific needs of various industries. For instance, an AI-driven customer service bot may be beneficial for retail, while predictive maintenance might be more appropriate for manufacturing.

Developing the AI Solution

- **Choose the Right Tools:** Leverage popular AI tools and platforms (such as TensorFlow, PyTorch, and cloud-based services like AWS and Google Cloud) to develop automation solutions.

- **Build Scalable Solutions:** Focus on creating automation systems that can scale with a client's business. Solutions should be flexible and customizable to adapt to different operational workflows.

- **Ensure Integration with Existing Systems:** Ensure that your AI-powered solution integrates seamlessly with the client's existing software, hardware, or databases, minimizing disruption and facilitating a smooth adoption process.

Packaging and Pricing AI Solutions

- **Software as a Service (SaaS) Model:** Offer your automation solutions on a subscription basis, providing businesses with ongoing access to updates and support. This model helps ensure long-term revenue.

- **Custom Solutions:** For larger companies or those with specific needs, offer custom AI solutions that are tailored to their operations, charging a one-time development fee or an ongoing service fee.

- Freemium Models: For smaller businesses or startups, consider offering a basic version of your solution for free or at a lower price, with the option to upgrade to more advanced features.

Building Long-Term Relationships with Business Clients

- Providing Excellent Customer Support

- Ongoing Training and Education: Offer training sessions and educational resources to help clients maximize the value of their AI automation solutions.

- Responsive Support: Provide a reliable support system for troubleshooting and queries, ensuring clients feel confident in using the technology.

- Proactive Communication: Stay in touch with clients through regular check-ins, offering updates, system improvements, and new features that may benefit their business.

Monitoring and Continuous Improvement

- Performance Tracking: Regularly assess how well the AI automation is performing for the client. Use data-driven insights to suggest improvements and optimizations.

- Update and Refine Solutions: As AI technology evolves, make sure your solutions stay up-to-date with the latest advancements. Offer regular updates and optimizations to keep your clients' systems running smoothly.

- Solicit Client Feedback: Encourage clients to provide feedback on the automation solution's performance, usability, and impact on their business. This feedback can help you improve the solution and foster a sense of partnership.

Building a Reputation for Trust and Reliability

- Demonstrating ROI: Regularly provide clients with reports and data showing how AI automation has improved their business performance, from time savings to increased sales or reduced errors.

- Referral Programs: Encourage satisfied clients to refer your services to other businesses by offering incentives or discounts for successful referrals.

- Long-Term Partnerships: Position yourself as a long-term partner by understanding the evolving needs of your clients and offering solutions that grow with their business.

Conclusion: The Future of AI in Business Automation

AI automation is rapidly becoming a core driver of business efficiency and growth across multiple industries. As the technology continues to advance, businesses will increasingly rely on AI to reduce operational costs, improve decision-making, and enhance customer experiences. By developing AI-powered automation solutions, entrepreneurs and businesses can tap into an ever-growing market with vast potential. Building strong client relationships, offering customized solutions, and continuously improving your offerings will ensure long-term success in the AI automation space.

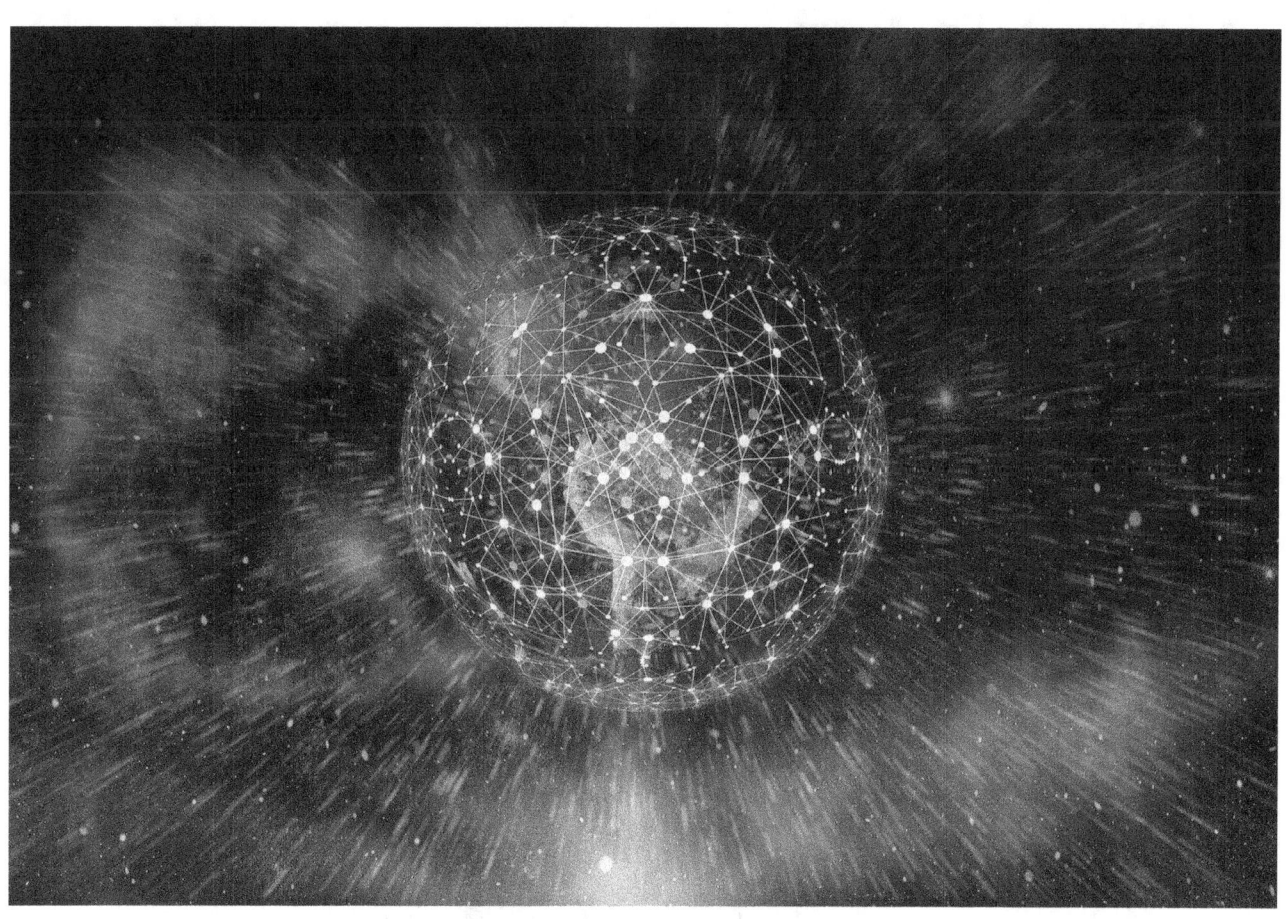

Conclusion: Unlocking the Potential of AI for Profit

As we've explored throughout this book, the opportunities to make money with AI are vast, dynamic, and continually evolving. From creating AI-powered applications and offering AI-driven services, to investing in cutting-edge startups and monetizing AI-generated content, the potential to leverage artificial intelligence for profit is unparalleled. Let's recap the **ten ways** to monetize AI:

1. **Building AI-Powered Applications** – Develop applications that utilize AI to enhance user experiences, whether through chatbots, recommendation engines, or custom solutions for businesses.
2. **Selling AI-Driven Services** – Offer services like AI consulting, automation, and optimization to help businesses improve operations and increase efficiency.
3. **Creating and Selling AI Content** – Use AI to generate creative content such as blog posts, videos, and social media content, and monetize through various online platforms.
4. **Developing AI Courses and Educational Materials** – Share your knowledge of AI by creating educational content and training courses to help others learn and apply AI.
5. **Investing in AI Startups and Technologies** – Explore opportunities to invest in AI ventures, focusing on promising startups and groundbreaking technologies that have the potential for high returns.
6. **Leveraging AI for E-commerce** – Integrate AI into your e-commerce business to optimize product recommendations, customer service, and inventory management.

1. **Monetizing AI-Generated Art and Media** – Create and sell AI-generated art, music, and multimedia, tapping into the growing demand for unique, tech-powered creative works.
2. **Developing Niche AI Tools** – Identify underserved niches and develop specialized AI tools that cater to specific business needs or industries.
3. **Using AI for Stock Market Analysis and Trading** – Leverage AI to analyze financial data and make informed investment decisions, or use AI-powered trading platforms for automated stock market trading.
4. **Offering AI Automation for Businesses** – Develop and sell AI-powered automation solutions that streamline business processes, saving time and money for your clients.

Taking Action: Start Monetizing AI Today

The power of AI is in your hands, and the opportunities are waiting for you to seize them. Whether you're just starting out in AI or are looking to expand your existing knowledge and skills, there's no better time than now to dive into this exciting field. The world of AI is growing rapidly, and by acting today, you can position yourself at the forefront of this technological revolution.

Get started now by focusing on one or two of the strategies outlined in this book that align with your strengths, interests, and resources. Take the first step—whether that's learning a new AI tool, developing a course, or launching your first AI-powered service. The key is to begin, experiment, and refine as you go.

The possibilities are endless, and your path to success with AI starts now.

Resources and Further Reading for Continuous Learning

To continue your journey in monetizing AI, here are a few valuable resources for further learning:

1. **Online AI Courses**:
    - **Coursera** (AI for Everyone by Andrew Ng)
    - **Udemy** (AI & Machine Learning for Business Professionals)
    - **edX** (Introduction to Artificial Intelligence)
2. **Books on AI and Business**:
    - *"Artificial Intelligence: A Guide for Thinking Humans"* by Melanie Mitchell
    - *"Machine Learning for Dummies"* by John Paul Mueller and Luca Massaron
    - *"AI Superpowers"* by Kai-Fu Lee
3. **AI Communities and Forums**:
    - **AI Stack Exchange** – A community-driven platform to ask questions and share knowledge.
    - **Reddit AI Community** – Participate in discussions with AI enthusiasts and professionals.
    - **Kaggle** – A platform for data science competitions where you can learn and practice AI with real-world data.

1. **AI Tools and Platforms**:
    - **Google Cloud AI** – Provides a range of AI tools for building applications and solutions.
    - **TensorFlow** – An open-source framework for machine learning and AI development.
    - **OpenAI** – Access tools like GPT models for building applications and services.
2. **AI News and Updates**:
    - **MIT Technology Review** – Stay up to date with the latest trends in AI and technology.
    - **AI Weekly** – A curated newsletter that provides AI news and updates.
    - **TechCrunch AI Section** – Follow the latest innovations and breakthroughs in AI.

By leveraging these resources, you can stay informed, sharpen your skills, and continue to grow your AI expertise. The future of AI is bright, and with continued learning and dedication, you can successfully tap into its vast potential to create meaningful income and business opportunities.

Embrace AI, take action, and watch as your entrepreneurial vision transforms into reality.

www.ingramcontent.com/pod-product-compliance
Lightning Source LLC
Chambersburg PA
CBHW082254220526
45469CB00009B/3005